ITIL® 2011 At a Glance

John O. Long

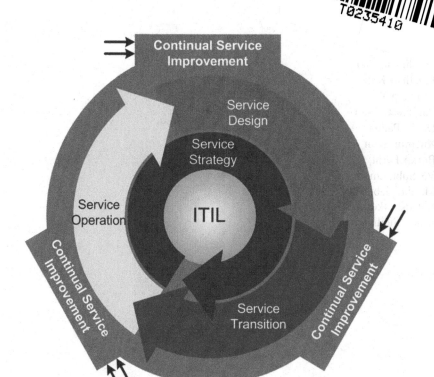

SpringerBriefs in Computer Science

Series Editors
Stan Zdonik
Peng Ning
Shashi Shekhar
Jonathan Katz
Xindong Wu
Lakhmi C. Jain
David Padua
Xuemin Shen
Borko Furht
VS Subrahmanian
Martial Hebert
Katsushi Ikeuchi
Bruno Siciliano

For further volumes:
http://www.springer.com/series/10028

John O. Long

ITIL® 2011 At a Glance

 Springer

John O. Long
Raleigh, NC, USA
johnoflong@gmail.com

ISSN 2191-5768 ISSN 2191-5776 (electronic)
ISBN 978-1-4614-3896-0 ISBN 978-1-4614-3897-7 (eBook)
DOI 10.1007/978-1-4614-3897-7
Springer New York Heidelberg Dordrecht London

Library of Congress Control Number: 2012939343

Printed on acid-free paper

Springer is part of Springer Science+Business Media (www.springer.com)

Copyright and Legal Information

Table of Contents

Introduction

Purpose

This book is designed as a quick reference for ITIL® 2011. It is not intended as an overview of ITIL® 2011 but merely as a memory jogger. It is suggested that you first familiarize yourself with the ITIL® 2011 documentation before using this book. This book contains references to more detailed material found in ITIL® 2011.

Audience

This book is intended to be used by anyone involved in planning, consulting, implementing, or testing an ITIL® 2011 implementation.

Organization of the Book

This book summarizes each of the ITIL® 2011 books. Each book in the ITIL® 2011 series represents a single stage in the lifecycle of an IT service. The first and last books in the series, Service Strategy and Continual Service Improvement, do not contain rigorously-defined processes, but instead describe a set of practices that may be used during those stages of the service lifecycle. The second, third, and fourth books in the series, Service Design, Service Transition, and Service Operation, contain rigorously-defined processes.

The subsequent chapters in this book each summarize one of the ITIL® 2011 books. The Service Strategy and Continual Service Improvement chapters contain the following structure:

- Brief Description of the Stage
- Overview Diagram of the Stage
- Key Concepts of the Stage
- Processes

Each process section within a chapter is structured in the following way:

- Process Purpose – The rationale for the process

J.O. Long, *ITIL® 2011 At a Glance*, SpringerBriefs in Computer Science, DOI 10.1007/978-1-4614-3897-7_1, © The Author 2012

- Overview Diagram – Shows all triggers, inputs, outputs, activities, and roles for the process

- Key Concepts – Various diagrams for describing important concepts and a list of key terms

- BPMN Workflow – The high-level workflow for the ITIL activities cast in very basic BPMN (Business Process Modeling Notation)

- Architecture Considerations – Changes that could be made to the process if a rigorously-defined ITSM architecture was needed. This is the view of the author based on inconsistencies and issues found with implementing ITIL 2011.

For more information

The author may be contacted at johnoflong@gmail.com

List of ITIL Processes

Process name	Acronym	ITIL Book	What's new in ITIL 2011
Access Management	ACC	Operation	
Availability Management	AVM	Design	
Business Relationship Management	BRM	Strategy	New process
Capacity Management	CAP	Design	
Change Evaluation	CHE	Transition	Previously known as "Evaluation"
Change Management	CHA	Transition	Build and Test Authorization separate from Deployment authorization
Demand Management	DEM	Strategy	Newly defined activities
Design Coordination	DES	Design	New process
Event Management	EVE	Operation	Workflow improved
Financial Management for IT Services	FIN	Strategy	Newly defined activities
Incident Management	INC	Operation	
IT Service Continuity Management	SCO	Design	
Knowledge Management	KNO	Transition	
Problem Management	PRB	Operation	
Release and Deployment Management	RDM	Transition	Some activities consolidated into Deployment
Request Fulfillment	REQ	Operation	Workflow improved
Service Asset and Configuration Management	SAC	Transition	
Service Catalog Management	SCA	Design	
Service Level Management	SLM	Design	Workflow improved

J.O. Long, *ITIL® 2011 At a Glance*, SpringerBriefs in Computer Science, DOI 10.1007/978-1-4614-3897-7_2, © The Author 2012

Service Portfolio Management	SPM	Strategy	Newly defined activities
Service Validation and Testing	SVT	Transition	
Seven-Step Improvement	SSI	CSI	Workflow improved
Strategy Management for IT Services	STM	Strategy	New process
Supplier Management	SUP	Design	New repository for data
Transition Planning and Support	TPS	Transition	

Service Strategy

Brief Description

Service Strategy describes an IT organization's high-level approach to providing services. First, the IT organization must identify the market for its services. This, in turn, drives the identification of services offerings as well as the strategic assets that will constitute those services. Envisioned services will be added to the service portfolio. These identified services will continue to be pursued until they are finally chartered for design (and development), which moves those services into the Service Design stage.

Supporting this overall activity is the need to determine the IT organization's overall approach to providing services. This may include internal providers, external providers, a shared approach, preferred providers, etc. In addition, several practices play a part in determining the overall service strategy, including financial management, demand management, and risk management.

J.O. Long, *ITIL® 2011 At a Glance*, SpringerBriefs in Computer Science, DOI 10.1007/978-1-4614-3897-7_3, © The Author 2012

Overview Diagram

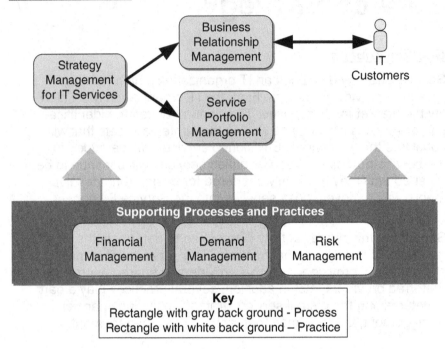

Service strategy defines a number of processes and practices

Service Strategy Key Concepts

Service Design Package and Other Service Artifacts

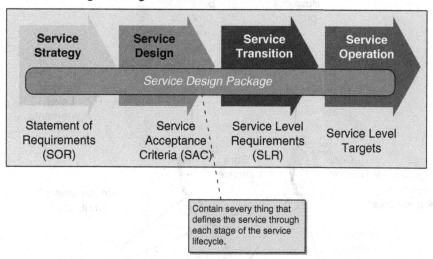

The service design package is used throughout the service lifecycle

Types of Services

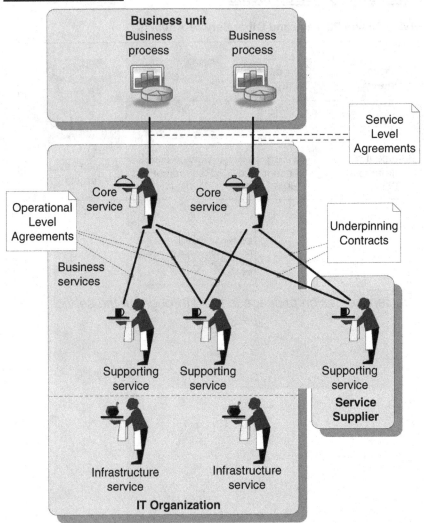

An IT organization provides core services, supporting services, and infrastructure services

Service Providers

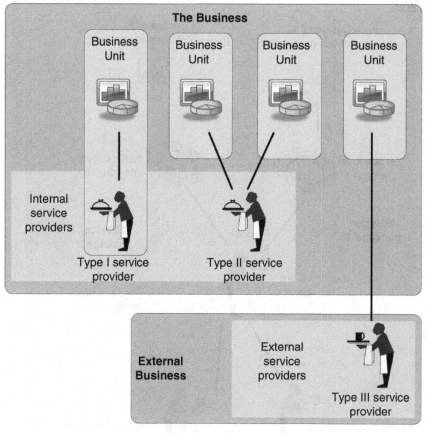

There are three types of service providers

Service Packages, Service Level Packages, and Lines of Service

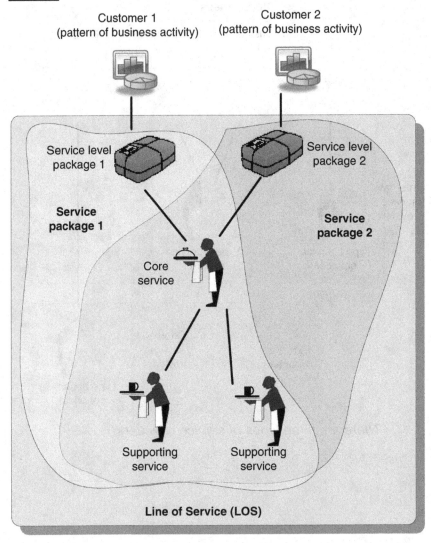

A line of service consists of all service packages for a service

Service Portfolio and Catalog

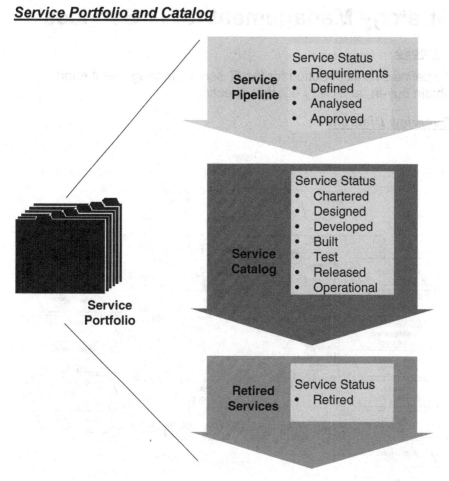

Service Pipeline

Service Status
- Requirements
- Defined
- Analysed
- Approved

Service Catalog

Service Status
- Chartered
- Designed
- Developed
- Built
- Test
- Released
- Operational

Service Portfolio

Retired Services

Service Status
- Retired

The service portfolio includes the service pipeline, the service catalog, and retired services

Strategy Management for IT Services

Purpose

To define overall direction for the IT service management effort, obtain buy-in, and carry out that direction.

Overview Diagram

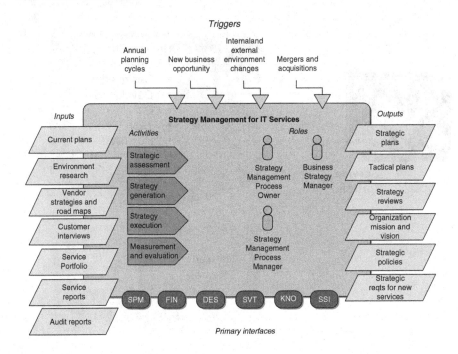

Key Concepts

Strategy – A high-level approach to carrying out defined IT objectives.

Sourcing Strategy – An overall plan and approach to how IT services are provided by internal and external service providers, specifically showing whether there is a preference for internal or external providers.

BPMN Workflow

Architecture Considerations

This process was originally a loosely-defined set of activities in ITIL v3 but has now evolved to a full-blown process. Strategy Management is a needed process, but is still defined at a very high level. More work needs to be done to make this process actionable.

Service Portfolio Management

Purpose

To manage and control the set of planned, existing, and retired IT services.

Overview Diagram

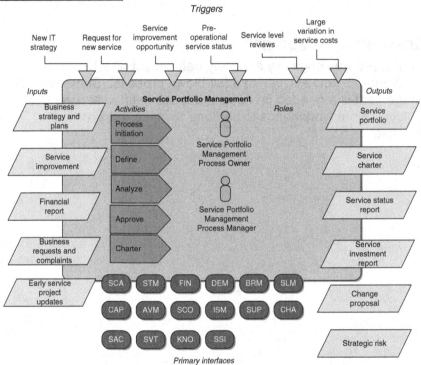

Key Concepts

Application portfolio – The entire set of IT applications, regardless of status in the application lifecycle. This may be implemented as part of the CMS or the service portfolio.

Customer agreement portfolio – The entire set of service agreements and other contracts between the service provider and its customers.

Customer portfolio – The entire set of customers who receive IT services from an IT service provider.

Market space – A description of the IT customer market, including a description of customer needs, that may be used to determine a set of IT services for that market.

Project portfolio – The entire set of IT projects, regardless of status in the project lifecycle.

Retired services – The subset of the service portfolio consisting of those services no longer available to customers.

Service catalog – The subset of the service portfolio consisting of those services currently available to customers.

Service model – A model of the interactions between service assets and customer assets within a service or set of services to create value to the customer.

Service pipeline – The subset of the service portfolio consisting of those services not yet available to customers.

Service portfolio – The entire set of services managed by a service provider, regardless of status in the service lifecycle.

BPMN Workflow

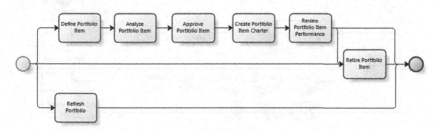

Architecture Considerations

This process focuses on the management of the Service Portfolio. However, there are other portfolios to be managed as well, including the Customer Portfolio, Customer Agreement Portfolio, Application Portfolio, and Project Portfolio. This process could be improved by being renamed to "IT Portfolio Management" and the scope broadened to manage all portfolios.

Financial Management for IT Services

Purpose

Obtain and steward financial resources for IT service management. This includes charging and billing IT customers as well as performing general accounting.

Overview Diagram

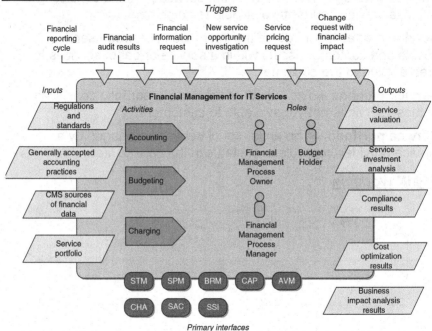

Key Concepts

Charging policy – A policy that defines how services and other items will be calculated and charged.

Charging process – The approach for deciding how to charge customers and bill them.

Cost center – An organization or project against which IT costs are expensed. Using this approach, IT customers are not charged for services. IT service providers can be paid for using either a cost center or a profit center.

Cost unit – Things that can be easily counted while assigning costs for a service. Cost units are the smallest items that can be counted within a cost element. For example, within the cost element "training", cost units could be instructors, training manuals, or meals.

Enterprise Financial Management – Financial management applied to the entire enterprise. Financial management for IT services is a subset of enterprise financial management.

External funding – Funding that is obtained from services sold to external customers.

Financial Year – A consecutive 12 month accounting period.

Funding model – An approach to how and when funding is available for a service provider. Funding models include rolling plan funding, trigger-based funding, and zero-based funding.

Internal funding – Funding that is obtained from other business units in the same organization.

Profit center – A business unit that charges for IT services. A service provider can be organized as either a profit center or a cost center. A profit center can charge to make a profit, operate at a loss, or just cover costs.

Rolling plan funding – A funding plan for a fixed length of time (i.e., cycle) and is used repeatedly for additional cycles. This type of funding is typically used for specific projects.

Trigger-based funding – A funding plan that initiates when a specific event occurs, such as a request to upgrade a service.

Zero-based funding – A funding plan that allocates costs to a specific budget amount, then recovers those costs from costs transfers from other business units. This is the most typical funding plan for IT services.

BPMN Workflow

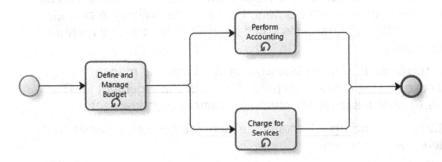

Architecture Considerations

Financial Management is a part of any major organization. ITIL calls this Financial Management for IT Services to distinguish it from other types of Financial Management within the enterprise. Although this is a useful distinction, the same could be said of many other ITIL processes. For instance, Change Management is a process found in many areas of the enterprise, not just IT, yet ITIL does not call that process "Change Management for IT Services". The phrase "for IT Services" should merely be an implied part of each ITIL process.

An important part of Financial Management not described in ITIL is advisory aspects of Financial Management such as providing financial assessments for change requests, financial feasibility to new projects or portfolio proposals, etc.

Demand Management

Purpose

Promote reduced demand for services as required by the IT organization. This may include reducing user access, providing user incentives to reduce demand during peak hours, etc.

Overview Diagram

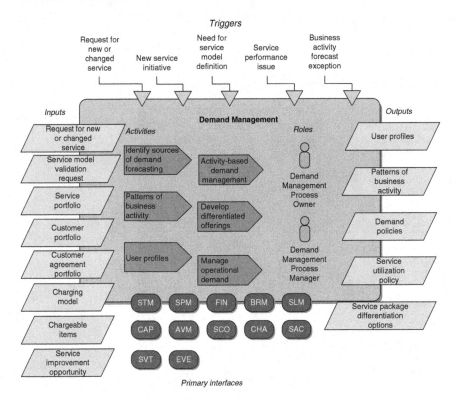

Key Concepts

Demand – A strong request for a resource, such as a service

Supply and demand – The principle upon which Demand Management exists – matching service supply to customer demand, including understanding potential demand and managing service assets to meet that demand.

Gearing service assets – The principle of adjusting service assets to meet the changing patterns of customer demand.

BPMN Workflow

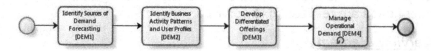

Architecture Considerations

Demand Management should include an activity to forecast demand management, not just look at past patterns of user behavior. There should also be an activity to report on demand management outcomes.

Business Relationship Management

Purpose

To develop and maintain business relationships between IT service providers and the IT customer, including ensuring that customer needs are realized in IT services.

Overview Diagram

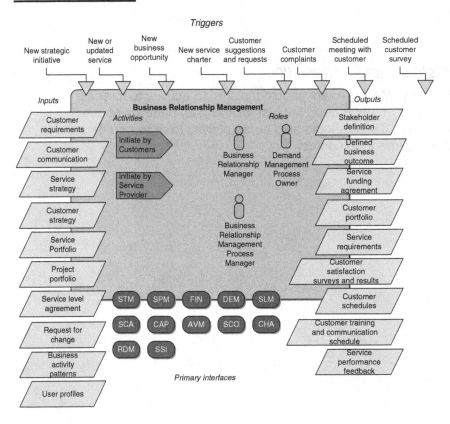

Key Concepts

Business Relationship Management Process vs Business Relationship Manager Role – The process is focused on maintaining appropriate relationships between the IT organization and its customers and service providers. However, the role is often involved in representing other processes with customers, such as Service Level Management and Service Portfolio Management.

Customer Satisfaction – The practice of taking actions to meet and exceed customer expectations.

Service Requirements – Customer wants and needs related to an IT service.

Complaint – Negative feedback from a customer that is an important input to continual service improvement.

Compliment – Positive feedback from a customer that is an important input to continual service improvement.

BPMN Workflow

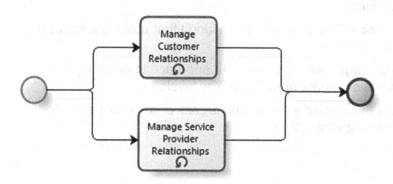

Architecture Considerations

As a new ITIL process, Business Relationship Management needs more architectural rigor. The two ill-named activities do not adequately describe the kinds of work that must be done in Business Relationship Management, such as identifying contacts, managing contact information, defining customer and service provider considers, monitoring and tracking issues, etc.

Other Practices

Risk Management – Identifying, evaluating, and determining acceptable responses to risks.

Organizational Change – The transition of an organization from a current state to a future state. At an enterprise level, this is often referred to as Change Management, not to be confused with ITIL (and other) Change Management.

Six Sigma – A data-driven methodology for reducing defects to near-zero.

Program and Project Management – The processes for initiating, coordinating, and monitoring ongoing programs and time-limited projects.

Governance – The approach to ensuring that policies and strategy are adhered to.

Quality Management System – An approach to ensuring that an organization meets targeted quality levels.

Balanced Scorecard – A tool that breaks down a strategy into key performance indicators.

Service Design

Brief Description

Service Design is a stage in the service lifecycle in which a new or modified service is developed and made ready for the Service Transition stage.

The primary effort of this stage is the design (and development) of the service. This include defining service requirements, designing the service solution, evaluating alternate suppliers of the service, and integrating existing service assets or creating them from scratch into a service.

Service Level Management provides the interface to IT customers in the collection of requirements. Supporting processes such as Availability Management, Capacity Management, Information Security Management, and IT Service Continuity Management are consulted to make sure the envisioned service will meet service level targets and expectations. Supplier Management manages relationships with potential service providers.

As the service progresses through this stage, the Service Catalog is updated with new information about the service, including status changes in the service. The Service Catalog is that part of the Service Portfolio that can be viewed by IT customers. It is also an instrument of Service Level Management to enter into discussions with IT customers about new service requirements or about the initiation of a service level agreement.

J.O. Long, *ITIL® 2011 At a Glance*, SpringerBriefs in Computer Science,
DOI 10.1007/978-1-4614-3897-7_4, © The Author 2012

Overview Diagram

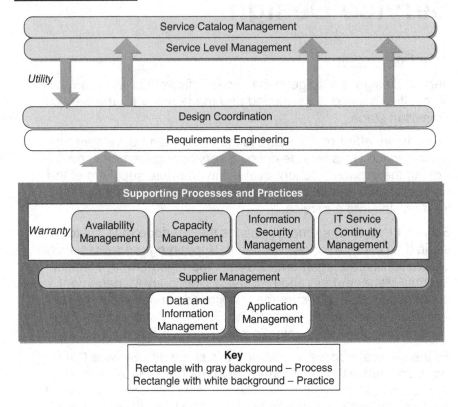

The design of services is at the heart of this lifecycle stage

Service Design Key Concepts

Service Availability

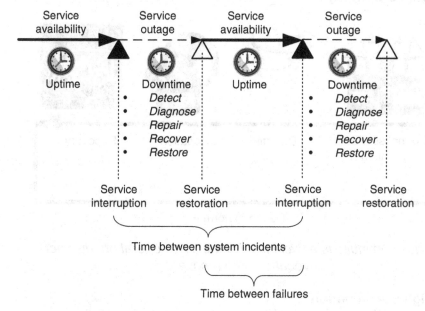

Several standard metrics are used to measure service availability

Information Security

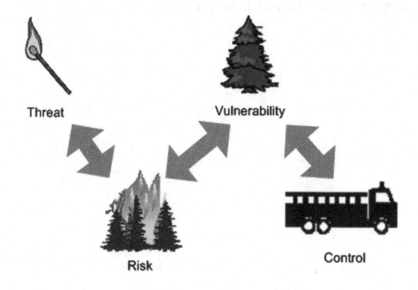

Information security involves identifying threats, vulnerabilities, and risks, and then implementing appropriate controls

Service Continuity

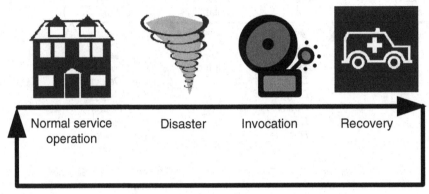

Normal service operation   Disaster   Invocation   Recovery

Return to normal

Service continuity is a cycle involving service operation, disaster, invocation, and recovery

Design Coordination

Purpose

Coordinate all service design work, including planning, resourcing, compliance, and handoff to service transition.

Overview Diagram

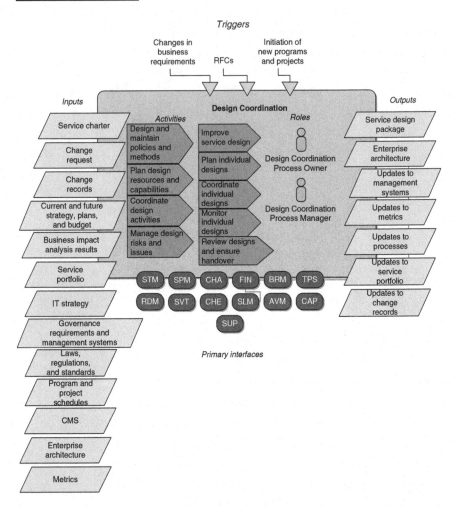

Key Concepts

Service – A collection of IT systems, components, and resources that work together to provide value to IT customers.

Service Design Package – The collection of all information and documentation about a service through each stage of its life cycle. There is a new service design package whether the service is new, updated, or retired.

Design balance – The goal of Design Coordination, which is an equilibrium of utility, warranty, standards compliance, and efficiency in developing and delivering the service.

BPMN Workflow

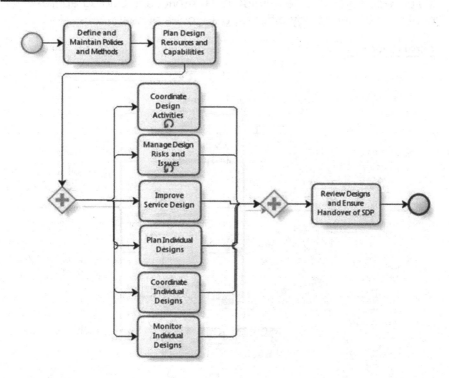

Architecture Considerations

Design Coordination, a new ITIL process, is not a well-recognized industry process. It seems to have been created because there was no overall process for managing the development of services or other IT products. This process should be replaced by a Product Management or Service Product Management process which defines the product vision, manages overall product development, determines when updates or new releases are needed, and ensures deployed products are kept at the right service level.

Service Catalog Management

Purpose

To provide and manage catalog of IT services, including appropriate views needed by different categories of customers.

Overview Diagram

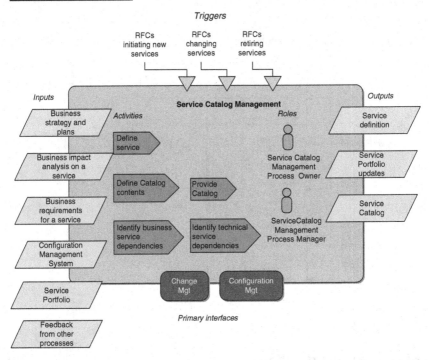

Key Concepts

Business Service Catalog – The collection of IT services that directly enable processes that are part of the business.

Hierarchy of services – A network of services that support business processes (business services) and services that enable those business services (technical services).

Service – A collection of IT systems, components, and resources that work together to provide value to IT customers.

Service Catalog – The collection of IT services currently provided to IT customers.

Service Package – An in-depth description of an IT service available through the Service Catalog.

Service Portfolio – The collection of all IT services, including those in the pipeline, those currently being delivered, and those that have been retired.

Technical Service Catalog – The collection of IT services that support business processes.

Types of service – A qualification of the services in the service catalog. Services should be put into different categories. The most useful categories are customer-facing services and supporting services.

BPMN Workflow

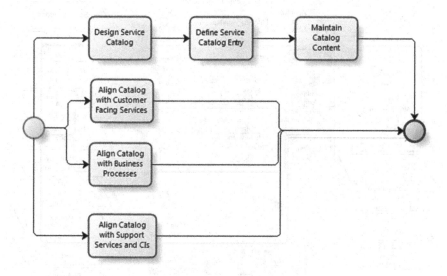

Service Catalog Management

Service Catalog Management exists primarily because of the prominence of the Service Catalog within ITIL. In reality, Service Catalog Management is nothing more than the administration and management of an IT application. If this line of thinking were carried through, there would be processes for administration of applications such as the CMDB, the Service Desk, the Operations Bridge, or others.

Service Level Management

Purpose

Ensure that an agreed level of service is provided to IT customers.

Overview Diagram

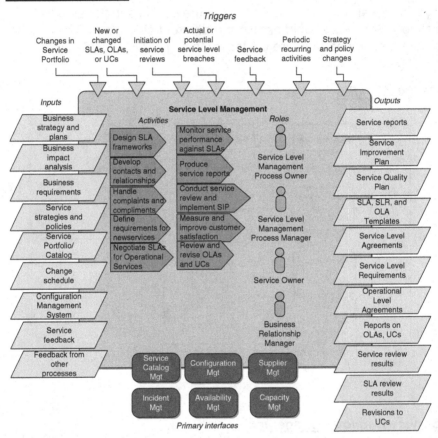

Key Concepts

Operational Level Agreement (OLA) – An agreement with an internal service provider to provide services within specified levels.

Service Level Agreement (SLA) – A negotiated agreement between the IT service provider and the IT customer defining the responsibilities of each party concerning the delivery of an IT service.

Underpinning Contract (UC) – An agreement with an external service provider to provide services within specified levels.

BPMN Workflow

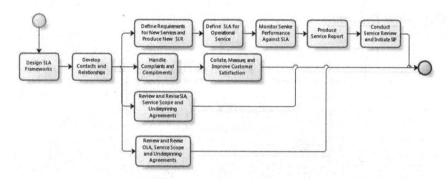

Architecture Considerations

Service Level Management, as defined in ITIL, suffers from having too many activities. These should be reduced a bit, since five to seven activities are typically about right for comprehensibility to a broad audience.

However, the process also suffers from the fact that there are two primary types of work being carried out in the process. The first type is the establishment of a service level agreement with a customer plus the accompanying work, such as creating OLAs and underpinning contracts, monitoring the service levels, and carrying out service reviews. The second type of work is responding to complaints, improving customer satisfaction, and developing relationships. This second type of work actually overlaps with Business Relationship Management and should be relegated to that process.

One ITIL-defined activity, Defining SLA Frameworks, is actually the kind of work that should go into the definition and setup of that process. Every process in ITIL should have an activity to define and implement process roles, work product templates, metrics, procedures, etc. but that kind of work is generally missing.

Capacity Management

Purpose

Provide a focal point for performance and capacity-related analyses and planning.

Overview Diagram

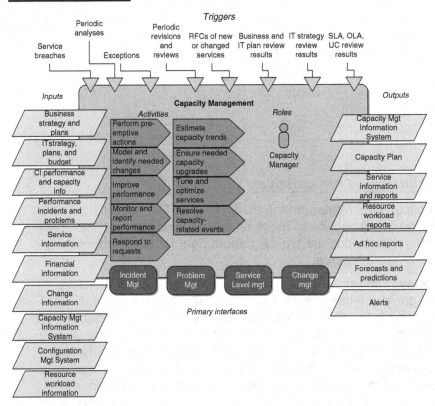

Key Concepts

Business Capacity Management – The management of capacity for business services.

Capacity – The maximum throughput provided by a CI

Capacity Plan – A long-term plan for providing adequate service capacity to meet expected service level targets.

Capacity Management Information System – The information system that contains all capacity-related plans, analyses, information, and reports.

Component Capacity Management – The management of capacity for configuration items that make up an IT service.

Demand – Desired use of an IT service or resource.

Human resource capacity – An aspect of Capacity Management that deals with staffing, scheduling, and training of human resources and their effects on service capacity.

Performance – The measurable results of a resource, CI, or service.

Service Capacity Management – The management of capacity for IT services.

Threshold – An operational level that, when exceeded, causes an alert or action to be initiated.

Tuning – The adjustment or manipulation of IT resources to make better use of those resources, including balancing and optimization.

Utilization – The use of a resource.

BPMN Workflow

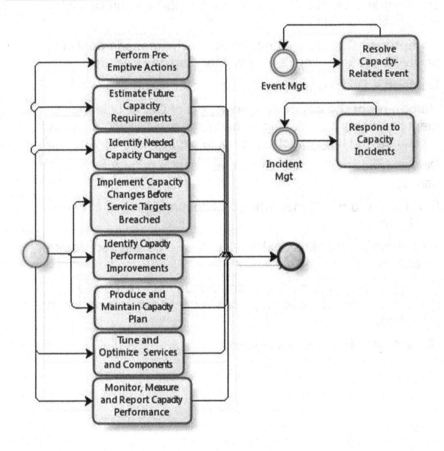

Architecture Considerations

Capacity Management lacks the kind of single-thread work found in Incident Management, which is typically responding to individual incidents. Instead, Capacity Management primarily carries out planning and responding to a variety of capacity-related requests. The activities prescribed by ITIL overlap and should be refactored so the activities can be better sequenced.

Availability Management

Purpose

Ensure that IT services meet service level availability targets, including planning for future service availability.

Overview Diagram

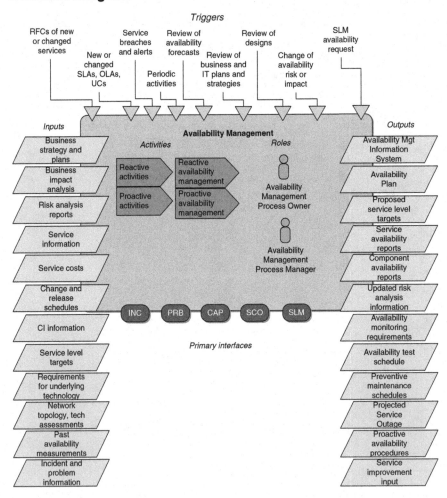

Key Concepts

Availability – The ability of an item to perform its function when required.

Component Failure Impact Analysis – Analysis performed to determine how component failure impacts IT services.

Fault Tree Analysis – Analysis that indicates a chain of events that led to a problem.

Maintainability – How rapidly an item can be restored to normal operation after a failure

Reliability – How long an item can perform its function without interruption

Serviceability – The ability of a third-party supplier to meet its agreed-upon service targets.

Service Failure Analysis – Analysis performed to determine the cause of related service interruptions. Note that this focuses on service interruption as opposed to root cause Analysis, which focuses on the cause of incidents.

Single Point of Failure (SPOF) – A configuration item that, when it fails, may cause an incident. Identification of SPOFs is an important aspect of managing service availability.

Vital business function – The critical business functions of a business service

Unavailability – The characteristic of a service when it is not available to users

BPMN Workflow

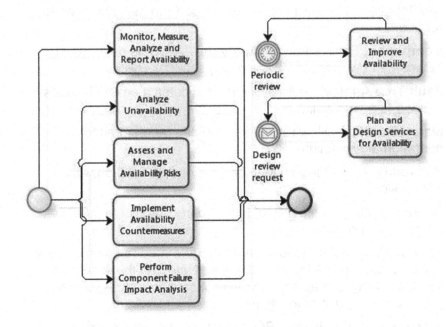

Architecture Considerations

Architecture Management has many similarities with Capacity Management, but is better architected by ITIL in that there are fewer activities. However, it suffers from the fact that most of the work is planning and responding to various requests. This makes it difficult to create a sequenceable workflow.

IT Service Continuity Management

Purpose

Ensure that IT services will continue to operate according to an agreed-to plan.

Overview Diagram

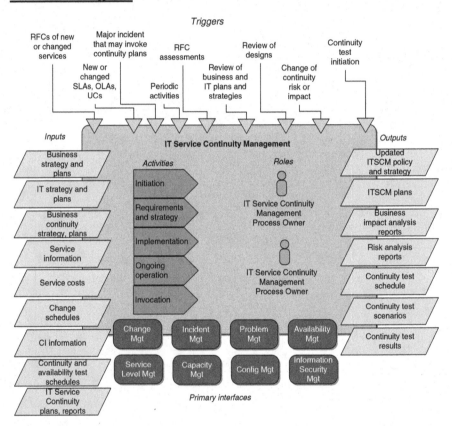

Key Concepts

Business Continuity – Continuing to provide business services after a major outage. This is directly related to IT Service Continuity.

Business Continuity Plan – A plan to restore business services after a major outage

Business impact analysis – An approach to determining vital business functions and dependencies.

Continuity testing – Performing tests of continuity plans to ensure that they will work in the face of a major outage.

IT Service Continuity – Continuing to provide technical services after a major outage.

IT Service Continuity Plan – A plan to restore IT services after a major outage.

Management of Risk (M_o_R) – A methodology to assess the impact of risks within an enterprise.

Restoration – Returning a CI or service to its normal operating state after repair and recovery.

Risk analysis – Determining the vulnerability to IT service threats.

BPMN Workflow

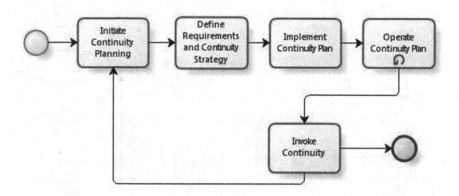

Architecture Considerations

This process is fairly well-architected by ITIL but is missing the activities to restore services from a continuity state to the normal state.

Information Security Management

Purpose

Align IT security with business security.

Overview Diagram

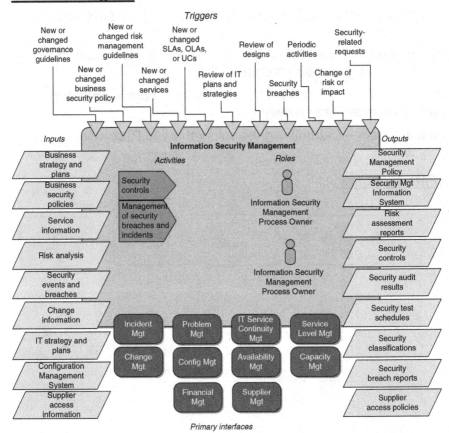

Key Concepts

Information Security Management System (ISMS) – An information system containing information security standards, policies, and procedures. An ISMS should support the following elements: Control, Plan, Implement, Evaluate, and Maintain.

Information Security Policy – An overall policy for conducting information security, supported by a number of underpinning security policies, including

- Access control

- Password control

- Antivirus policy

- Internet policy

- Asset use policy

- And others

ISO 27001 – International standard for certifying an ISMS

Risk Assessment – Assessment of security risks must be carried out in order to achieve the objectives of ISM.

BPMN Workflow

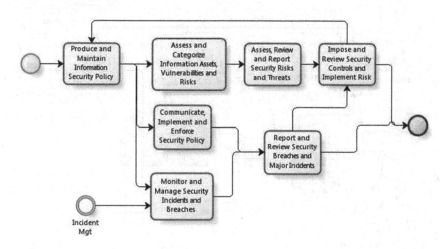

Architecture Considerations

The majority of the activities in this process involve analysis/planning activities, but a smaller number of activities involve operational work focused on security incidents. These latter activities overlap with activities in Incident Management.

Supplier Management

Purpose

Manage service providers in support of service level targets.

Overview Diagram

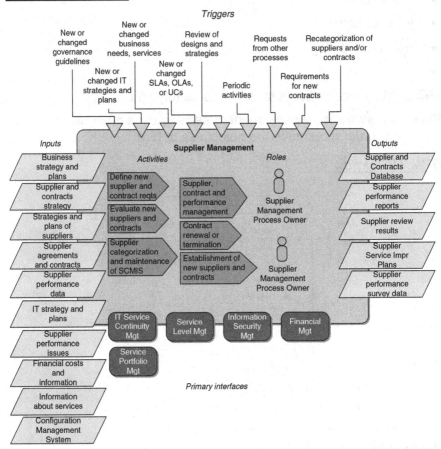

Key Concepts

Invitation to Tender (ITT) – A document similar to the Statement of Requirements

Operational Level Agreement (OLA) – See Service Level Management.

Service Provider – Any internal or external provider of an IT service

Statement of Requirements (SoR) – A document identifying all requirements for a service or project

Supplier and Contracts Database – a repository of information about suppliers and contracts with suppliers

Supplier performance – Suppliers that provide services at appropriate levels of service tend to be retained, whereas those that do not tend to have their contracts terminated

Supplier Service Improvement Plan – Actions that are to be taken by a supplier to improve their levels of service

Underpinning Contract (UC) – See Service Level Management.

BPMN Workflow

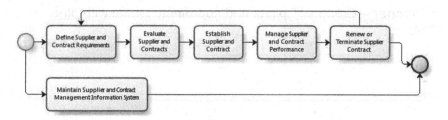

Architecture Considerations

This activities in this process were structured to represent the life cycle of a supplier relationship, from establishing a supplier contract, through managing the ongoing relationship, to the end of the supplier contract. Unfortunately, the process does not cover procurement from the supplier, which is missing from ITIL altogether. Procurement should be a part of this process.

In addition, this process contains an activity to manage the Supplier and Contract Management Information System. This is an inconsistency, since most of the other processes do not contain an activity to manage the primary process tool/repository.

Other Practices

Application Management – The management and control of applications through their entire lifecycle, from creation to retirement.

Data and Information Management – The control, organization, and disposition of data and information within the organization. This includes collection as well as disposal.

Requirements Engineering – The discipline of collecting, organizing, and prioritizing requirements for a CI or service to be designed.

Additional Service Design Roles

IT Designer/Architect – Designs needed IT technology and coordinates those designs within the IT organization

IT Planner – Creates IT plans and coordinates them with other IT plans

Service Transition

Brief Description

The service transition stage readies a new or changed service for operation. The primary activity done during this stage is Transition Planning and Support. This process plans all of the activities that must take place to put the service into production. This may involve the creation of a number of RFCs that will carry out all necessary changes (Change Management) and deployments (Release and Deployment Management).

Prior to moving the service into production, there may be a period of testing and validating the service to ensure sufficient quality of the service.

An overall evaluation framework is used by transition planning and support to determine if the service is still in an acceptable state to proceed or must be remediated in some manner.

As the service is readied for production, various configuration items and assets must be assembled and configured. Information about all of these CIs and assets, as well as the relationships between all of these elements, must be maintained in order to provide the best support for the service.

Knowledge about the services and underlying CIs and service assets is collected during this stage and subsequent stages in order to provide effective support for service faults.

J.O. Long, *ITIL® 2011 At a Glance*, SpringerBriefs in Computer Science,
DOI 10.1007/978-1-4614-3897-7_5, © The Author 2012

Overview Diagram

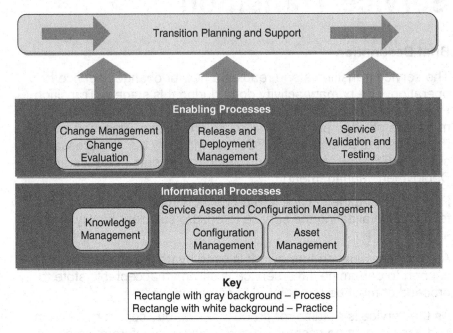

A number of enabling and informational processes support the transition of a service into operational status

Service Transition Key Concepts

Stakeholder – Any party that has an interest in a service, configuration item, or other IT asset that may be subject to change.

Service Knowledge Management System

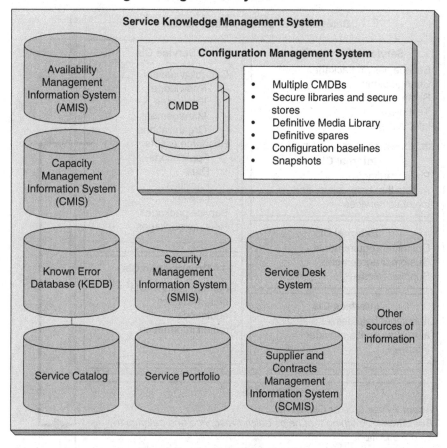

The service knowledge management system includes many
service management information systems

Configuration Items (and Assets)

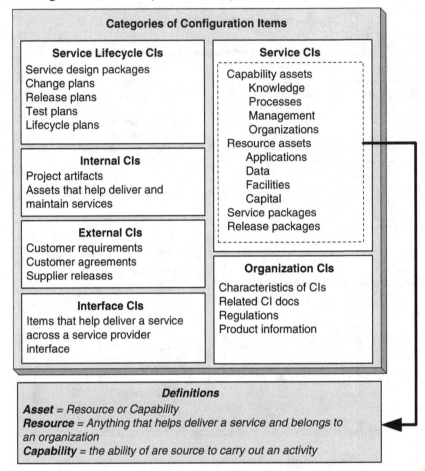

Categories of Configuration Items

Service Lifecycle CIs

Service design packages
Change plans
Release plans
Test plans
Lifecycle plans

Internal CIs

Project artifacts
Assets that help deliver and
maintain services

External CIs

Customer requirements
Customer agreements
Supplier releases

Interface CIs

Items that help deliver a service
across a service provider
interface

Service CIs

Capability assets
  Knowledge
  Processes
  Management
  Organizations
Resource assets
  Applications
  Data
  Facilities
  Capital
Service packages
Release packages

Organization CIs

Characteristics of CIs
Related CI docs
Regulations
Product information

Definitions

Asset = Resource or Capability
Resource = Anything that helps deliver a service and belongs to
an organization
Capability = the ability of are source to carry out an activity

There are a variety of different types of CIs and assets

Change

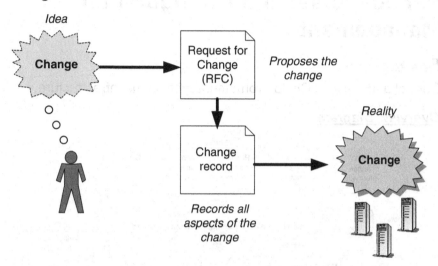

Proposed changes are RFCs whereas change records record everything about proposed and implemented changes

Release

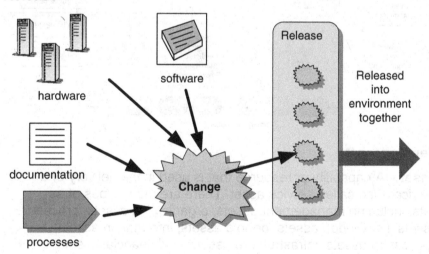

A release may include a number of changes

Service Asset and Configuration Management

Purpose

Control and track all CIs to promote integrity in the infrastructure.

Overview Diagram

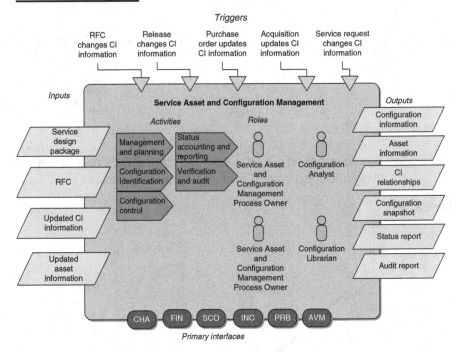

Key Concepts

Asset – A capability or resource that is used in the delivery of a service. Also called service asset. There are many types of assets, including management assets, organization assets, process assets, knowledge assets, people assets, information assets, application assets, infrastructure assets, and financial assets

Asset Management – The process within SACM that deals with inventory of all service assets

Configuration baseline – The configuration of a set of CIs that has been reviewed and agreed upon

Configuration item – An element of the IT infrastructure that is managed as part of the delivery of an IT service, including people, hardware, software, services, facilities, SLAs, and documentation.

Configuration Management – The process within SACM that ensures that configuration items within the IT infrastructure are identified, maintained, and properly controlled.

Configuration management database (CMDB) – A virtual repository of information about configuration items.

Configuration Management System (CMS) – A system of databases and tools that manage information in multiple CMDBs, as well as additional information related to CIs.

Configuration model – A depiction of the relationships between CIs

Configuration record – The record of information about a CI

Decommissioning assets – The work of removing an asset from service

Definitive Media Library (DML) – The secure library that stores definitive versions of all electronic CIs.

Definitive spares – A secure store for CIs that are at the same levels at CIs in a test or live environment.

Secure library – A secure storage of electronic assets. This is a part of the CMS.

Secure store – A physical storage location storing IT assets. This is a part of the CMS.

Snapshot – The status of a set of configuration items at a point in time

BPMN Workflow

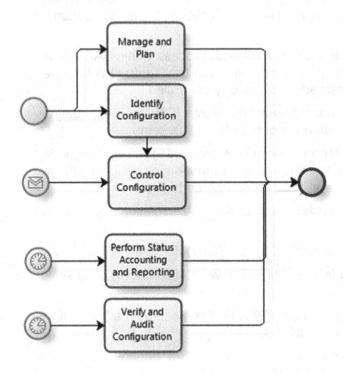

Architecture Guidelines

Service Asset and Configuration Management contains an activity called Manage and Plan which defines the process framework for Configuration Management. Every process should have an activity to define the process framework.

Change Management

Purpose

Manage all changes to the IT infrastructure in a controlled manner.

Overview Diagram

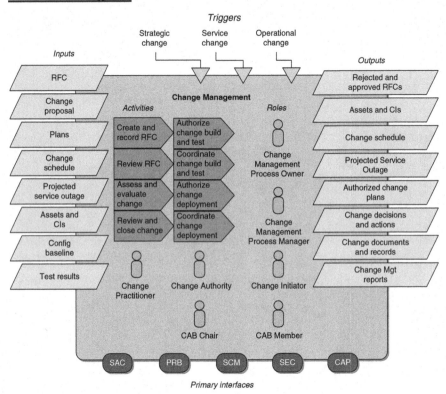

Key Concepts

Change assessment – An evaluation of the change request from various points of view.

Change authorization – Approval of a change request. There may be different authorization levels based on the type of change being considered.

Change priority – The order in which change request are considered for authorization

Change process model – Predefined workflows for changes that fit within a predetermined template

Change record – a record of a change throughout its lifecycle. This information becomes the initial part of a change record.

Remediation – The approach or plan to be followed if a change is not successful. This may involve backing out an installation, invoking continuity plans, or some other approach.

Request For Change (RFC) – A record of a proposed change

Risk categorization – An evaluation of the overall risk of a change request to the business Standard changes – A very low-risk change that is pre-authorized for implementation.

BPMN Workflow

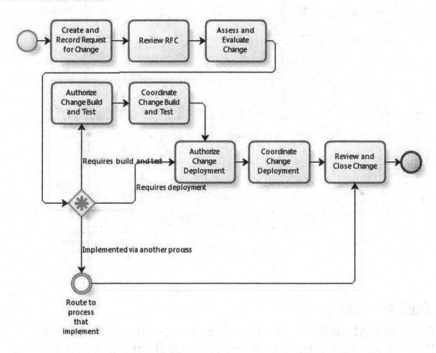

Architecture Considerations

This process should be combined with Change Evaluation, which has no purpose other than to support Change Management.

Release and Deployment Management

Purpose

Build, test, and deploy capabilities to provide services. This does not include application development.

Overview Diagram

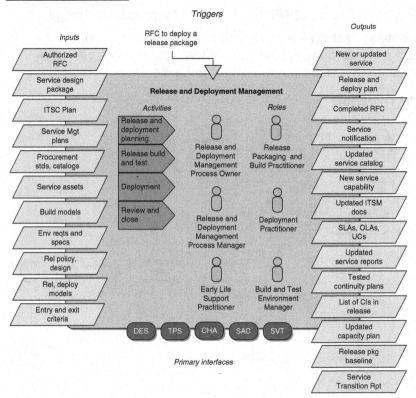

Key Concepts

Deployment option – The overall approach for deploying a release, such as gradually or in one large deployment.

Early life support – A period of additional attention and support for an IT service immediately after deployment. This consists of more intensive monitoring, adjustment of service level targets, and additional resources to handle related incidents and problems.

Pilot – Deployment of an IT service or asset that is limited for trial purposes.

Push approach/ pull approach – Different approaches to making a release package available to users. A push approach installs the release package for the user. A pull approach makes the release package available on a central website that may be downloaded and installed at the user's convenience.

Release – A group of changes that are tested, packaged, and deployed into the IT infrastructure at the same time. These changes may include hardware, software, documentation, or other items.

Release and deployment model – A standard or repeatable model for carrying out a release. There may be such models for different types of releases.

Release package – The set of configuration items in the release that will be built and deployed together.

Service rehearsal – A type of service testing that involves performing as much of the service as possible before actual deployment.

Service retirement and cleanup – Services or service assets may be retired as part of a deployment action.

Service transfer – Deployment may involve transfer of service from one service provider to another.

BPMN Workflow

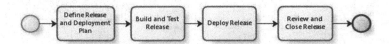

Architecture Considerations

This process should include the creation of a process framework to identify the overall approach to carrying out the process. In addition, an improvement activity should be included in the process.

Service Validation and Testing

Purpose

Ensure that a new or changed service will meet customer requirements and will be fit for purpose and fit for use.

Overview Diagram

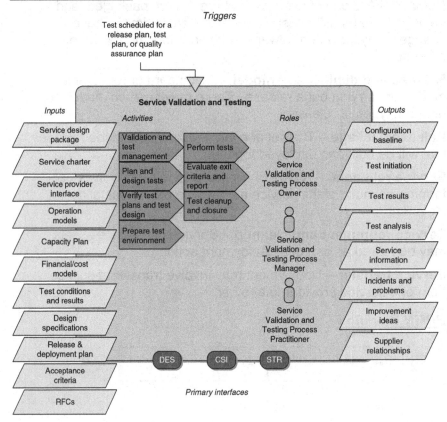

Key Concepts

Service Design Package – The documented requirements and design of a service.

Service level package – The level of utility and warranty that goes with a specific service package

Service model – A depiction of service functionality

Test model – A model of how to define each service deliverable.

Test Strategy – The general approach to carrying out testing.

Types of testing – Various aspects of what to test in a service, including usability, accessibility, performance, availability, compliance, remediation, etc.

Validation – the practice of identifying that a new or modified configuration item meets needs of the business.

Verification – the practice of identifying that a new or modified configuration item meets requirements

BPMN Workflow

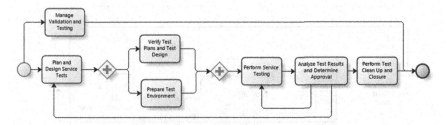

Architecture Considerations

Service Validation and Testing should be an integrated part of the solution development process. Typically, this would be an SDLC or waterfall development process. Most IT organizations already have such processes and do not need a separate Service Validation and Testing process.

Transition Planning and Support

Purpose

Plan service transitions that appear in each stage of an IT service's lifecycle, including design, transition, operation, and retirement.

Overview Diagram

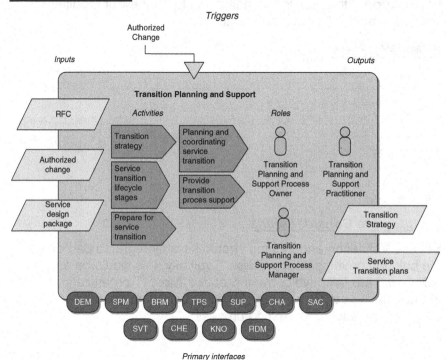

Primary interfaces

Key Concepts

Service Design Package – specifications, models, architectures, designs, plans, and acceptance criteria

Service Transition – a stage in the lifecycle of an IT service

BPMN Workflow

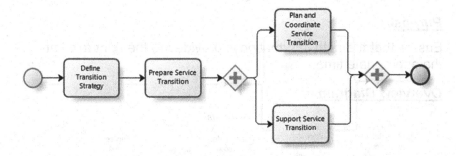

Architecture Considerations

A service transition is really just an IT project that coordinates a number of related changes. This process would be unnecessary if ITIL had a Project Management process.

Knowledge Management

Purpose

Ensure that the right information is provided to the right roles at the appropriate time.

Overview Diagram

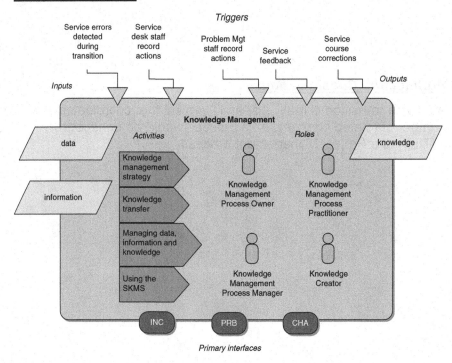

Key Concepts

Data – disjointed facts about events

Information – context for data

Knowledge – Insights gained from individuals about events concerning how events happened

Knowledge Management Strategy – Overall policies, governance, roles, and procedures for knowledge management

Service Knowledge Management System – The overall system that encompasses all Service Management Information Systems, including

- Availability Management Information System

- Capacity Management Information System

- Configuration Management System

- Known Errors Database

- Security Management Information System

- Supplier and Contracts Database

- and others

Wisdom – Discernment concerning why events happened

BPMN Workflow

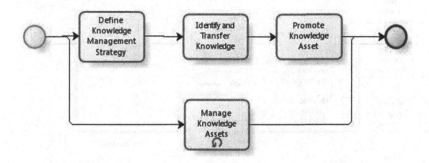

Architecture Considerations

The activity Manage Knowledge Assets spans a lot of work. This activity is integrated with the work of all other processes, since every process manages some type of knowledge.

Change Evaluation

Purpose

Determine the ramifications of a proposed service change whether as a result of a Request for Change, a new Service Design Package, or testing.

Overview Diagram

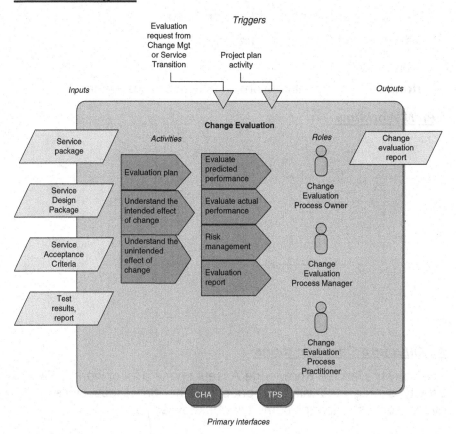

Key Concepts

Actual performance – A measure or assessment of the past effects of an implemented change.

Deviation – The determination that actual performance is acceptable

Predicted performance – A measure or assessment of the effects of a future change

Risk – A potential occurrence that may cause loss

Risk management formula – Likelihood x impact

Unintended effects – Side effects of a change, arrived at by discussions with stakeholders to determine effects other than those anticipated by the change request

BPMN Workflow

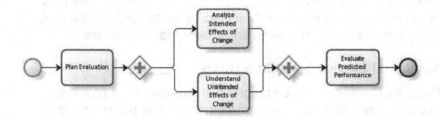

Architecture Considerations

This process should not exist as a separate process since it does not have an existence apart from Change Management. This process should be merged with Change Management.

Other Practices

Communications and Commitment Management – The practice of providing effective communication to all affected parties concerning a change.

Organizational and Stakeholder Change Management – The practice of managing process and cultural changes among IT stakeholders. Many changes affect important underpinnings of how an organization works. This practice goes beyond mere deployment of changes to determine how to improve the acceptance of significant changes within an organization.

Stakeholder Management – The practice of resolving the needs and concerns of stakeholders of IT services. Stakeholders may represent a variety of interests, including customers, users, regulatory organizations, business units, partners, and others.

Additional Service Transition Roles

Process Owner – Provides high-level direction for a process and ensures that a process is implemented and performed to support business objectives

Service Owner – Provides high-level responsibility for the design, development, maintenance, and support of a service

Service Operation

Brief Description

In the Service Operation stage, a service is available for IT end users. During execution of the service, it is monitored to determine service levels as well as to look for operational faults.

Operational faults may be detected as events from service monitoring. Those events may be resolved within Event Management or may be escalated to Incident Management to be resolved by Service Desk personnel. In either case, the event is recorded as an incident and the service is restored as quickly as possible via either a workaround or some other resolution.

Faults may also be detected by users, who may contact the Service Desk to log an incident. The Incident Management process is used by the Service Desk to get the service restored to the user as quickly as possible.

The Problem Management process supports the Incident Management process by looking for incident trends (problems) and resolving root causes of those problems. This process also proactively addresses any faults not yet previously identified.

The user may also contact the Service Desk to carry out simple, virtually risk-free actions (service requests) that cannot be performed by the user (Request Fulfillment) or to provide access to services or service assets (Access Management).

J.O. Long, *ITIL® 2011 At a Glance,* SpringerBriefs in Computer Science, DOI 10.1007/978-1-4614-3897-7_6, © The Author 2012

Overview Diagram

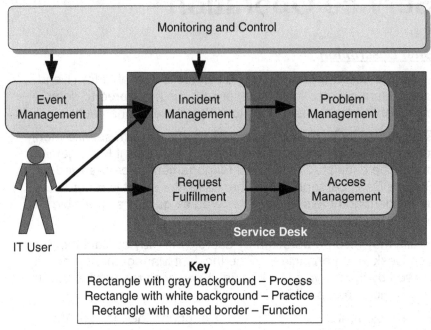

The service desk is at the heart of the service operation stage

Service Operation Key Concepts

Events, Incidents, and Problems

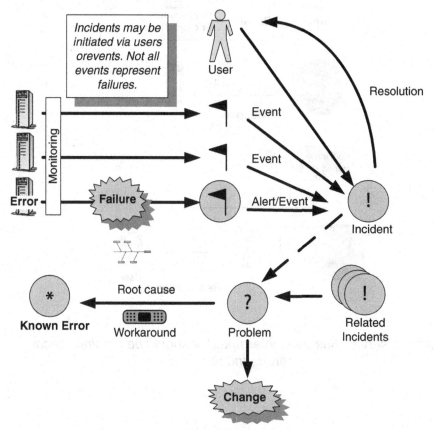

Events may turn into incidents, and related incidents may constitute a problem

Restoring a Service

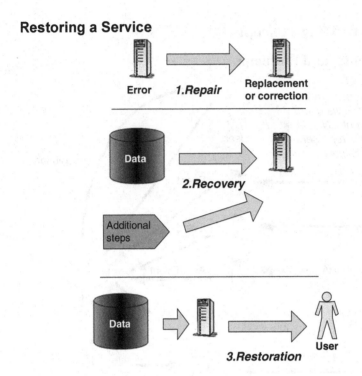

After a service has been interrupted, it should be repaired, recovered, and restored

Service Desk

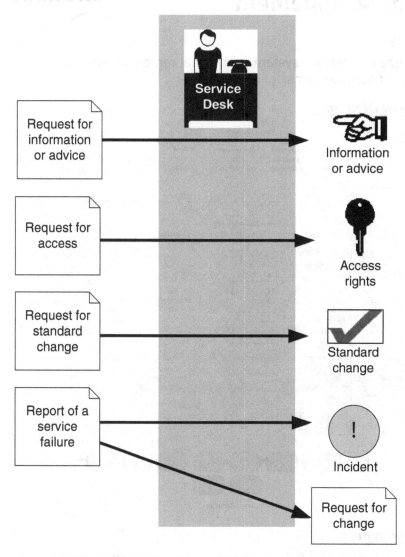

A user may submit a variety of things to the service desk which are then processed or routed to the appropriate team

Event Management

Purpose

To identify and resolve system events that represent failures within configuration items.

Overview Diagram

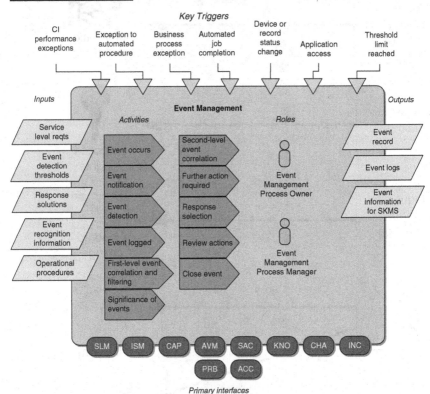

Primary interfaces

Key Concepts

Event Correlation – Various system monitoring tools generate events according to predefined event generation rules. The usefulness of event management is closely tied to how well these rules are defined. Tightly constrained rules will not generate enough events to identify many failures, whereas loosely constrained rules will generate many false positives.

Event Filtering – Ignoring events that are of less significance to focus on events of greater significance.

Event response – Some events may have an automatic response associated with the event, such as restarting a process. Other events may require manual intervention, such as incident management or creation of an RFC.

Event rule sets – Categories of rules defining how event messages are processed and evaluated.

Monitoring – Monitoring is different from event management. Monitoring determines the status of a configuration item or service, whereas event management identifies changes in status of those CIs and services that represent faults within the IT infrastructure.

Types of events – The three primary types of events include informational events (provides information only), warning events (unusual situations that do not warrant immediate action), and exception events (unusual situations that warrant immediate action).

BPMN Workflow

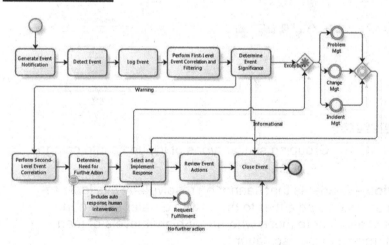

Architecture Considerations

Event Management has too many activities at the highest level.

Incident Management

Purpose

To restore service operation to a user as rapidly as possible.

Overview Diagram

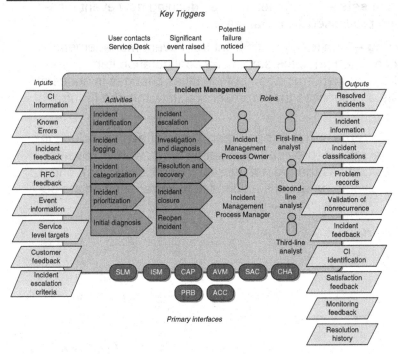

Key Concepts

Classification – Grouping similar types of incidents into categories.

Escalation – Incidents that cannot be resolved by available resources are escalated either to those with greater skills (functional escalation) or to those who are at higher levels of management (hierarchical escalation).

Incident models – Similar types of incidents may follow similar paths to resolution. For this reason, predefined workflows for specific types of incidents may be created.

Major incidents – Some incidents are of such magnitude that they are treated individually. Such an incident may be treated as an individual problem in Problem Management.

Prioritization – The relative impact and urgency of an incident, where impact is the effect the incident has on the business, and urgency is how long it will take for the incident to have that effect.

Recovery – Returning a configuration item to its working state after resolution

Repair – Replacing or fixing a configuration item

Resolution – Addressing the root cause of an incident or problem via a repair or a workaround.

Timescales – A time period in which an incident should be resolved or escalated. Because incident management is focused on rapid restoration of services, timescales are important.

BPMN Workflow

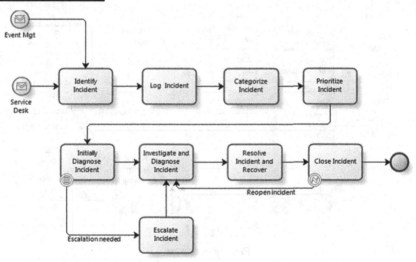

Architecture Considerations

Both categorizing and prioritizing incidents are closely related because they determine which team will respond to the incident and how quickly they will do so. These activities should be merged together to make room for other common activities such as creating the process framework and continuous improvement of the process.

Request Fulfillment

Purpose

Request fulfillment processes service requests and requests for information. Access-related service requests are processed by Access Management.

Overview Diagram

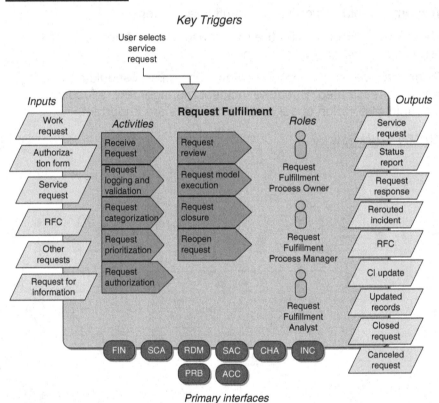

Primary interfaces

Key Concepts

Request Model – a predefined workflow for handling a specific type of service request

Service Request – a standard (preapproved) change that is straightforward and virtually risk-free.

BPMN Workflow

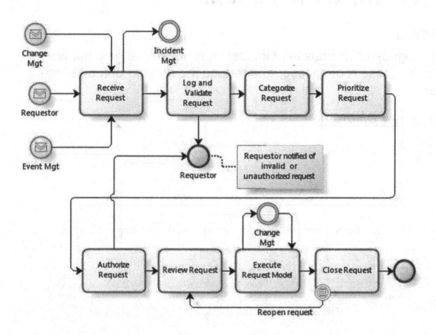

Architecture Considerations

ITIL has always suffered from the lack of a process that specifically serves as the front-end for the service desk. The Request Fulfillment should serve that purpose, but it is not explicitly described that way. This leads to all kinds of religious debates among ITIL adherents concerning whether Incident Management or Request Fulfillment is the first process to receive user contacts to the service desk. This process should be explicitly architected (and possibly renamed) so it is clear that all initial user contacts with the service desk come through this process.

Problem Management

Purpose

To diagnose root causes of incidents, request changes that will resolve those root causes, and reduce the number of future incidents.

Overview Diagram

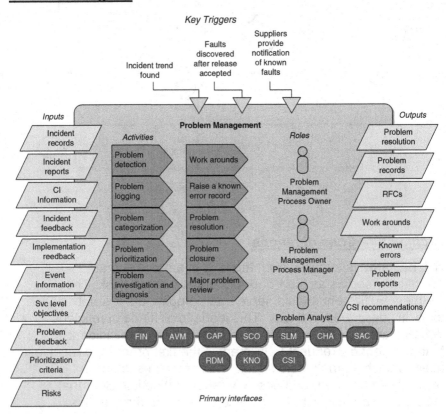

Key Concepts

Known Error – a problem for which the root cause has been determined and a workaround or resolution has been created.

Proactive problem management – looking for potential problems before they are reported by other processes or functions and resolving those problems.

Problem – a problem is a root cause of a group of related incidents.

Problem Model – a predefined workflow for handling a specific type of problem

Reactive problem management – resolving problems that have already been uncovered by incident management or some other source.

BPMN Workflow

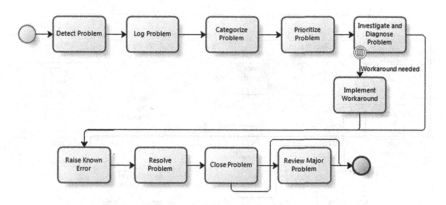

Architecture Considerations

This is a fairly well-architected process.

Access Management

Purpose

To provide rights for a user to access a service.

Overview Diagram

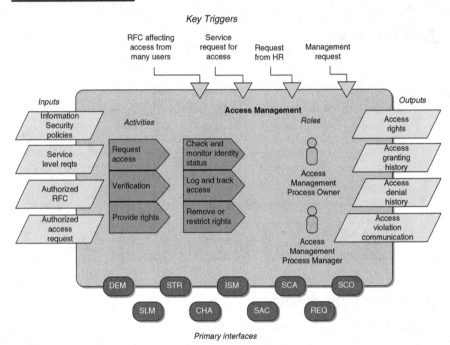

Key Concepts

Access – the ability to make use of a specific configuration item. There may be different types of access, such as read, write, execute, etc.

Directory services – An application that records the rights given to each identity and allows modifications to those rights.

Identity – the name of a user or group. Access rights are granted to identities.

Rights – permission given to an identity.

BPMN Workflow

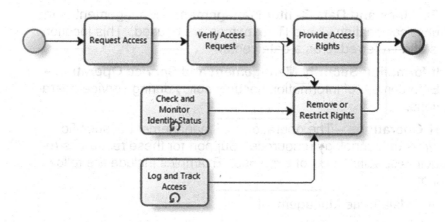

Architecture Considerations

There needs to be more support for managing user identitities. Two specific areas that should be addressed include the following:

- Periodically, there is a need to audit user identities and determine if there are any that need to be removed. Users sometimes leave the organization without their identity being removed. Also, duplicate or temporary identities may exist that are no longer needed.

- Group identities need to be managed, as group members typically change over time.

Other Practices

Facilities and Data Center Management – Management of the physical location where IT resources are housed. This location is often referred to as a data center.

Information Security Management and Service Operation – Enforcement of information security policy during service operations.

IT Operations – The operation and management of specific types of technology resources. Support for these resources requires specific types of expertise. Examples include the following:

- Mainframe Management
- Server Management and Support
- Network Management
- Storage and Archive
- Database Administration
- Directory Services Management
- Desktop Support
- Middleware Management
- Internet/Web Management

Monitoring and Control – The cycle of service monitoring and response.

Service Operation Functions

A "function" is an abstract organizational unit within an IT organization. It represents a real organization or group, but not a process. A function may use one or more IT processes or practices to carry out its objectives. There are five primary functions within Service Operation, some, of which, are divided into smaller functions.

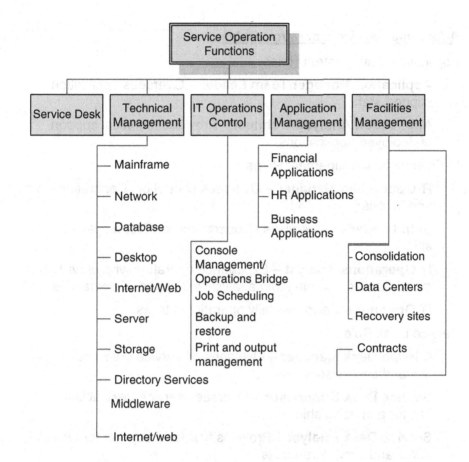

Service operation functions

Application Management – Control of the entire lifecycle of an application

Facilities Management – Management of IT data centers and other physical IT facilities

IT Operations Management – Ongoing operation and execution of IT services and IT resources in support of those services

Service Desk – User support for IT services

Technical Management – Provides specialized technical skills to carry out IT operations

Additional Service Operation Roles

Application Management Roles

Application Manager/Team Leader – Oversees application support staff

Application Analyst/Architect – Provides technical support of deployed applications

IT Operations Management Roles

IT Operations Manager – Oversees control of IT operations and facilities

Shift Leader – Supervises IT operations staff for a specific shift

IT Operations Analyst – Experience operators who provide more detailed planning and analysis in support of operations

IT Operator – Performs daily operational tasks

Service Desk Roles

Service Desk Manager – Oversees all service desk activities and supervisors

Service Desk Supervisor – Oversees service desk activities for a specific shift

Service Desk Analyst – Provides first-level support for incidents and service requests

Super User – Users who act as liaison between the service desk and the user community

Technical Management Roles

Technical Manager/Team Leader – Provides leadership for a technical team

Technical Analyst/Architect – Determine stakeholder needs for a technical domain and provides analysis in support of that technical domain

Technical Operator – Performs daily technical operations tasks

Continual Service Improvement

Brief Description

During the Continual Service Improvement stage, the IT organization collects data and feedback from users, customers, stakeholders, and other sources to enhance services and how they are provided.

This involves the use of a seven-step improvement process that collects data, analyzes the data, provides recommendations, and implements those recommendations.

In support of the improvement process, Service Level Management collects information from IT users and customers and data from the operation of the services. Service measurement and reporting provides standard vehicles for describing the performance of the services.

Finally, all service improvements must be scrutinized according to whether they meet the needs of the business and provide an overall return on investment.

J.O. Long, *ITIL® 2011 At a Glance*, SpringerBriefs in Computer Science, DOI 10.1007/978-1-4614-3897-7_7, © The Author 2012

<u>Overview Diagram</u>

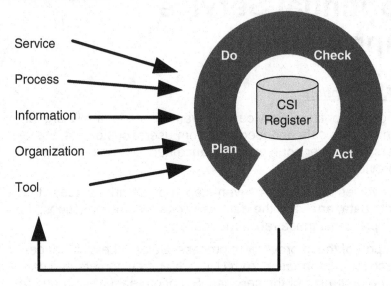

*A variety of ongoing processes support the Continual
Service Improvement lifecycle stage*

Seven-Step Improvement Process

Purpose

To guide improvement efforts related to IT services, processes, organizations, information, and tools.

Overview Diagram

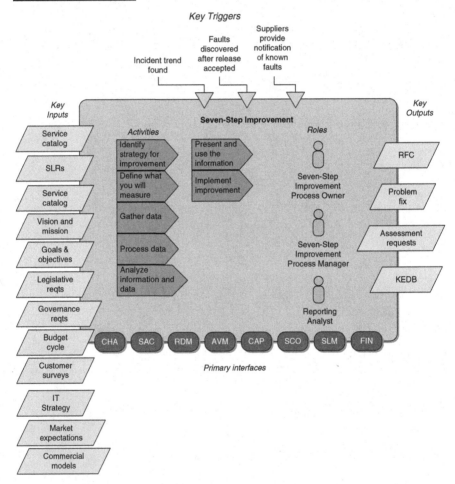

Key Concepts

Plan Do Check Act (PDCA) – The key stages of the quality improvement cycle. PDCA is also known as the Deming Cycle.

CSI Register – A repository of all improvement efforts.

BPMN Workflow

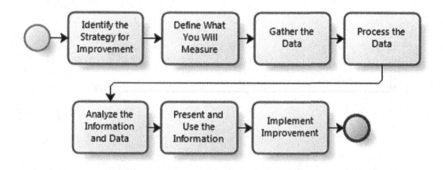

Architecture Considerations

The Seven Step Improvement Process is a generic process that can be applied to any context. It is unfortunate that an entire book is devoted to this process. Other improvement processes exist in other context that are just as suitable. Every other process should have an improvement activity that assesses the process and looks for ways to improve it. Therefore, this improvement cycle should be built into every other process.

Additional CSI Roles

Business Relationship Manager – See the chapter on Business Relationship Management.